GW00673147

EXPLAINING
What the Bible says about Money

DAVID PAWSON

ANCHOR RECORDINGS

Copyright © 2016 David Pawson

The right of David Pawson to be identified as author of this
Work has been asserted by him in accordance with the
Copyright, Designs and Patents Act 1988.

First published in Great Britain in 2016 by
Anchor Recordings Ltd
Synegis House, 21 Crockhamwell Road,
Woodley, Reading RG5 3LE

No part of this publication may be reproduced or transmitted
in any form or by any means, electronic or mechanical,
including photocopy, recording or any information storage
and retrieval system, without prior permission
in writing from the publisher.

**For more of David Pawson's teaching,
including DVDs and CDs, go to
www.davidpawson.com**

**FOR FREE DOWNLOADS
www.davidpawson.org**

**For further information,
email: info@davidpawsonministry.com**

ISBN 978-1-911173-35-9

Printed by Lightning Source

This booklet is based on a talk. Originating as it does from the spoken word, its style will be found by many readers to be somewhat different from my usual written style. It is hoped that this will not detract from the substance of the biblical teaching found here.

As always, I ask the reader to compare everything I say or write with what is written in the Bible and, if at any point a conflict is found, always to rely upon the clear teaching of scripture.

David Pawson

EXPLAINING
What the Bible says about Money

This booklet is about a practical subject that is of interest to those who work in the marketplace, and that is money. Jesus actually said more about money than about salvation, prayer, heaven or anything spiritual. He knew that money was a very real part of people's lives, and that is why he said more about money than about any other subject.

Now money is basically a convenience. That is why it was invented. Smaller communities up to that point made their exchanges in barter. You would produce too much butter and somebody else would produce too much meat, so you exchange some of your surplus butter for their surplus meat. That is how the world was organised for a long time.

Money was invented in the eastern part of Turkey, which was then called Asia. The king who started it all was King Croesus. He has gone down in history as having eventually been a very rich man. When you look geographically at the place where money first appeared, don't read too much into this but it was right next door to where Satan had his headquarters on earth. If you go to Pergamum, a town in the east of Turkey, and climb the steep hill on the top of which you find the old town and the theatres and the libraries of that place, you will find the bare site of Satan's seat. It has gone now – it is in Germany, in the Pergamum museum in Berlin.

You ought to go and see it. It is an incredible temple to the king of all the gods. It is in the shape of a huge armchair with steps leading up to it. It really is an impressive thing. When you have climbed the steps, there were columns on three sides like a great armchair. In the middle was an altar where they kept a fire burning to Zeus day and night. The top of this hill is about a thousand feet above the modern town and could be seen for miles. This was where Satan had his headquarters.

Satan can't be everywhere. He has agents everywhere, but that is where he had his headquarters in the days of the New Testament. When you study the letter to the seven churches in Revelation, you find that Jesus spoke to the church at Pergamum, and he said, "I know where you are, where Satan's seat is." When you study the other six letters, you see that the character of those churches was related to the geographical distance from Satan's headquarters. It is quite fascinating. The two nearest churches were both corrupted by Satan from within the church. The next two nearest churches were suffering for their faith – the only two that Jesus had no criticism of. But they were suffering from pressure outside the church.

Of the two churches furthest away from Satan's headquarters, one had lost its first love and the other had grown cold. So the situation of the churches was directly related to their geographical distance from Satan's headquarters. I don't think Satan's headquarters is there now, and the whole temple was removed by a German archaeologist and rebuilt in Berlin. I found Christians in Berlin who were praying that it would be given back to the Turks because they believed that some bad influence came to Berlin with it. It came before both World Wars, which is interesting. Anyway, don't read too much into that. I just find it interesting and I like to share with people what is interesting. But let us get on with the subject.

So money was invented there, right next door to Satan's headquarters. If you ask me where his headquarters is now, I don't know. Although I am quite sure it is not there any more, that was the crucial area in New Testament days, where the biggest battle between the Church and the world, – between the two cultures – took place. If the battle was lost there, the Church would have been lost. I believe that is why Jesus wrote his only letters to the churches in that particular area, where Greek and Roman culture met the mystics of the east. It was right on the major road between Rome and Persia. It was the crucial area where everything crossed: business, commerce, everything happened there. The more you study that region the more you will see how crucial it was.

So money was invented in that region and it is simply a convenience – carrying a whole lot of butter in one pocket to change it for some meat is not very convenient. The world soon learned that commerce needed something else. It needed money, which is much more easily carried about and transferred from one place to another so that trading and commerce can carry on. But money is also easier to accumulate. When you build up your goods, moth and rust consume, there is always a decay in everything physical. But money gave you the power to accumulate it, and I am afraid also gave you power. Money is power, as we have learned to our cost.

Money talks not with an actual voice, but it speaks a great deal. It is absolutely important to Christians who handle money, and those who handle a lot of it, that it talks Christian language, and we are going to look at that in detail. Somebody has said, "Give me your bank accounts for the last few years and I will tell you what kind of a Christian you are." That is quite a challenge. It is probably the best test of our love for Jesus: how we handle our money, whether it be a small or large amount.

Many people go to work to get money. In my booklet on the subject of work, I pointed out that is legitimate. It is biblical to go to work and earn enough for yourself, your dependants and for the poor. That should be a desire of every Christian. Now as I affirmed earlier, Jesus says more about money than about any spiritual topic. There is more about money in the New Testament than many Christians would prefer. But before we look at what the Bible says about money, let us consider its place in the Western economy. I spoke on this subject in Singapore and include that in the Western economy because it is part of the Western cultural world. Frankly, I haven't been to many countries that display as much wealth as you see as you walk around Singapore. There is obviously plenty of money there and much has been spent on all sorts of wonderful things to attract tourists, which in turn, is one of its major incomes, having been a small country with few natural resources – and I was amazed at it. It is an economic miracle there how this little island should produce the culture that it has.

In the "Western" economy we are in what is called the "consumerism" culture. We are very conscious of it. Every time you turn on the television you are encouraged to get rich, to spend it too, and to spend it quickly. There is a lot of over-eating and over-drinking in Western culture, but no one seems to try to discourage over-getting or overspending when it comes to money. Our culture is geared to encouraging us to spend right up to our income and beyond it. Advertising is encouraging us to buy things that we don't need, but which we do want. One of the secrets of controlling money is to distinguish between what you want and what you need. I will come back to that when we get on to biblical teaching.

We are encouraged to spend money quickly. The advertising industry is not the easiest industry for a Christian to work in because at its heart is a manipulation of human desire, and it is very cleverly handled to make you want more than you have got. It is very easy to fall for it after you have watched some television commercials. You have very much liked to do what they have urged you to do. Otherwise they wouldn't show those commercials, if they didn't change people's appetites and habits. Companies pay a fortune to advertise precisely because they know they will change people's habits and introduce their wants rather than their needs into lives.

You know that people are manipulated in stores, shops, supermarkets, by the very positioning of things in the right place so that you will want to buy them. There are extra things that are just before you get to the check-out. The whole thing is a masterly manipulation of customers. We have got used to this in consumerism. We know how to sell stuff, how to encourage impulse buying, so that you come out of the shop with more than you intended when you went in. It is so very easy to be snatched up in a consumerist culture. It is all around us.

So many people live right up to and beyond their income. We are encouraged again and again in a credit society to spend money before we have got it. There is a snare there because it assumes that your income will go on at the same level. You are assuming that, and therefore that you will be able to pay it back. Then things happen to us beyond our control and we are not able to pay back what we have virtually borrowed on interest by using a credit card.

Society today is living on debt. Many individuals are, and the society in which they live are. I live in a country that is living on debt. We are borrowing from our children and grandchildren without their consent by living in the national debt. It will have to be repaid by our children, grandchildren and great-grandchildren. But we seem to have no conscience about borrowing without their consent from our descendants.

In Britain our government is borrowing over a thousand pounds for every person in Britain to maintain our standard of living. So a Christian in Britain can't help but live in debt. The nation is borrowing for the maintenance of a standard of living we have got used to. I am just trying to state facts. Recession hits a whole nation, and therefore the economy has become the major factor in our elections. At its simplest, people want to be better off all the time. We have got used to a standard of living that has steadily increased over the years and basically people will vote for a government that will go on lifting that standard of living.

But when the financial situation crashes, as it did a few years ago, the nation is torn in an election. On the one hand people want the standard of living to go up, but on the other hand there are people with enough sense who will vote for a government which will reduce the national debt. I think this genuinely happened at our last election. Whether our present government is able to do what it promised remains to be seen. But what has happened is that the standard of living of many people has gone down and the further it goes down the less they feel like voting for a government that will reduce the debt. We are torn now between the two motivations.

Behind all this is the "big lie". We need to nail that one straight away. The "big lie" is: "the secret of happiness is money". It is not true. But what we really want – freedom, security, power, respect – all demands money, according to the "big lie". The "big lie" is behind gambling advertising. It is saying: "You could be rich quickly for no effort other than buying a ticket." Since people long for security, freedom, respect and power, they fall for the advertising, which always concentrates on the rare winner and doesn't interview the many losers. But, as I have explained elsewhere, gambling is gaining at another's loss.

Now there are a number of aspects of money that I want to

teach about in the light of biblical teaching. Getting money, having money, or keeping money, spending money, and giving – the Bible has things to say about all those. It is a very comprehensive book when it comes to money. First of all, let us look at *getting* money. The basic principle of getting money for Christians is to earn it. Therefore, to exchange goods and services of equal value to the money received, that is earning. Getting your money from those who benefit from your labour – from your activity. That is a basic Christian duty: to earn money if you have the capacity to do so.

Unemployment is an evil that we should fight. There are too many people who can work but who don't have the opportunity to do so. It is rare for a country to have more jobs than people. Most countries in the world have more people than jobs now. Therefore earning becomes a real difficulty for many. It is obvious that we are not to earn our money at the expense of our bodies, minds, or spirits. If we are doing damage to any of those three things then God is not approving. To add to that, if we are employed in a job that is damaging other people's bodies, minds or spirits we should think again.

Of course, employment in an immoral or an illegal occupation is out for the Christian. The illegal drugs trade and the sex trade are out. What about other illegal employment? Law-abiding employment is in, but law-evading work is out. I am afraid there is quite a lot of that. Very clearly, Romans chapter 13 says we are to pay our taxes, for example. Tax avoidance and tax evasion are two different things. But the line between them is fairly delicate and not too clear.

I was recently in a country—I won't name it—where a Christian shared with me this problem. He was in employment on an average wage, but that country is a country where tax evasion is everywhere. Nobody fills in their tax returns honestly; everybody is fiddling with their taxes and it is well known. It is a game with the government.

Therefore nearly everybody is evading tax and they have set the level of income tax much higher than it should be, knowing perfectly well that the average citizen only declares half their income – therefore the need of the government for the tax is geared to that fact. If anyone is honest and declares their whole income, their tax bill is perhaps twice what is should be. A Christian man in ordinary employment under average wage said, "If I am honest in filling in my tax returns I couldn't afford to live."

Now what a dilemma! I said, "Why couldn't you afford to live?"

He replied, "Because the income tax is based on those who don't declare their income. So it's very much higher than it should be and the government is quite content. They know it's higher than it should be because they don't know the incomes. What should I do as a Christian?"

What would you advise that person to do? I felt terrible, but advised him to be honest and to trust God for the rest. But that is easy to say and I know it was hard for him to do. I said, "I think that is the Christian thing to do, and if every Christian in this country did that, perhaps the government might change their mind about how to get tax." But it would mean that he would have to trust the Lord far more than he had hitherto, because far too much of his legitimate income would be lost. But the scripture is clear that you pay taxes. Read Romans 13 carefully. You are under a duty to pray for the government – and that, under the dictatorship of the Roman emperor, was valid.

People say, "Well, I'll pray for those I've elected and put in," but there they have been told to pray for those who had not been elected by the population, who were not their own choice. Pray for them and pay taxes. The Roman taxes were quite heavy, and yet Christians were exhorted to pay them gladly.

There are other jobs, which are illegal. I think there is some trading in commodities, and especially trading in money, that becomes very close to professional gambling and fulfil those three conditions of gambling which I have given elsewhere, and which I repeat here, because they are important. Gambling is an exchange of money without an exchange of goods or services, that is one thing. Secondly, it is gained by creating an artificial and unnecessary risk. Before you entered that financial situation you didn't have the risk of losing. Thirdly, it is always gaining at someone else's loss. Technically, gambling is only occurring where all three of those are happening together. But I know some jobs where all three do apply, and a Christian should not be getting his money in that kind of a job.

Insurance is minimising risk – a risk you already have, whether fire risk or accident risk, and it is right to pay your insurance on your driving a car because you are already facing a severe risk in driving and you are minimising that by sharing it with other drivers. That is not gambling, though people have often got them confused. Getting money from investments is not immoral or illegal. In fact, Jesus advised someone to put money in a bank and get some interest for it. That is simply when you have surplus money enabling other people to use it and benefitting from the benefits you have given them in investment.

But investment can certainly slip into gambling, especially if you are in and out of your investments quickly, because you are then playing the markets or "making a killing" (what an interesting phrase). Phrases like that indicate that you should think again about what you are doing. But the basic principle is clear: you don't live on charity; you don't live on other people; you don't beg. "Cannibalism" in the financial area is living off other people one way or another. You work for it with your hand or your head, and you are exchanging something of equal value to your wage or salary.

This applies also to Christian work – those who work for the Lord in preaching, teaching, evangelising. The Bible is absolutely clear they are working and they deserve a wage. "A labourer is worthy of his hire" – I am quoting Jesus there. Paul reiterated that and said that he was free not to take money from those who came to Christ through him because he didn't want them to get the wrong idea. But he said, "I have a right to income for myself and a wife it I had one." But it was a right he chose to forego.

There is no difference in the work we do. That is why, concerning elders in a congregation whose work is heavy and who labour in preaching and teaching (that is preaching to the unconverted and teaching the converted – that is the difference) – elders who labour in both those fields are worthy of a double—what? Your Bible probably says "honour". But the word is actually "honorarium". They are worthy of a double wage; they are working twice as hard in those two tasks. Then, in Galatians 6, Paul says, "It is right for you if you are grateful for spiritual ministry to reward those who have given it to you in material ways." So that would help enormously to reduce this idea that some people are in spiritual work and must live by faith, and others are on a salary or wage income. That has helped to divide people up into super-spiritual and ordinary Christian workers. We are all in the same category when it comes to work and money.

The temptation in modern society is quick profit: to make more money than you deserve so that you can retire early, or so that you have more money than you deserve to spend in other ways. The offer of easy money is quite a snare, quite a temptation. If you see an offer of very high interest that would enable you to double your money in ten years and get out of it, that is quite a temptation but it is a wrong one. Investment with unusually high rates of interest are to be suspected, and you need to do a bit of investigation before you touch them.

I am going straight on to having money, to keeping money, to building money up in your bank account. There is much in the Gospels about the dangers of being rich. I have to say I cannot see the biblical foundation for what is called the "health and wealth gospel" – that the Lord has promised that every believer will always be healthy and that his intention is to make every believer wealthy. That teaching is built on some very insecure foundations in scripture of a few texts here and there, interpreted one way. It is not the general teaching of scripture.

Take the whole Bible, and particularly the whole New Testament. There is a difference between the Testaments and an important one. Israel had no clear understanding of what happened after death. That comes out so many ways. What they had revealed to them was all concerned with this life. In the Psalms you will find phrases like: "The dead do not praise you." They believed that after you died you went to a shadowy place called "Sheol" where you slept in the Lord. Their favourite phrase for death was "fallen asleep". They had no concept of real life beyond the grave. So they had to learn in this life rewards and punishments, blessing and curses. So God cursed them physically and he blessed them physically. Abraham was a rich man and so were many others. Even so, the rich found great temptations. Solomon is a classic example, and he did not master his money. Immediately he died, the whole country split in civil war as the result of his spending and his taxing, which was way beyond what it should have been.

But in the New Testament, life and immortality have been brought to light and the resurrection has made a huge difference. The whole concept of life after death, which is only hinted at rarely in the Old Testament, is now central to the New Testament. Therefore, rewards for good living can be put into the new life, which is more real than life before death. That has meant a whole switch between Old and New Testaments in terms of rich rewards. I throw that in, check me out, but you'll find that there is a very great difference of dimension there, between the two Testaments.

Let us come back to *keeping* money. Making money in the right way, the temptation is to build it up and keep it. Is that wrong? There is more in the Gospels against being rich than we like to think. It is hard being rich. It is very hard for a rich man to enter the kingdom. But I am interested to know: is it hard being rich after you have got into the kingdom? The answer seems to be yes, very hard. There are dangers in having a lot of money. Christ himself didn't; he was a poor man, relatively speaking. Others gave to him, and Judas kept the money as the treasurer of the disciples. But you know what happened to Judas. He was tempted to sell Jesus for money. Thirty pieces of silver was the price of a slave. That meant that he could be one step up in society as a slave owner. What an amazing thing to do, for the treasurer of the disciples to want money more than his Lord. Now there have been all sorts of theories to excuse Judas which have been preached around the world, but what we learn in the Bible is that he began to love money. I believe we should take that as the final explanation – that is the one given by the Lord. But there are some theories that say he was trying to bring Jesus out as king; he was trying to force him to declare himself publicly and get on the job much more quickly, and there are all kinds of theories. But the Bible explanation is that money became just a bit too much for him. Church treasurers have been known to do the same – handling a lot of money is not easy. It carries its own temptations.

There are many, many New Testament references which favour the poor. In the beatitudes in Matthew, Jesus says,

"Blessed are the poor in spirit." But Luke's version of another sermon he preached says, "Blessed are you poor, and woe to you rich," and he meant not poor in spirit but poor in money and rich in money. When he said "Woe", that was a curse. "Blessed" is a blessing, but "Woe" is a curse. We should be careful not to use that word. I have heard parents say to their children, "You'd better do that or woe betide you." They little realise that they are cursing their children. We have to be careful what we say.

But Jesus both blessed and cursed people. For every "blessed" he added a "woe" in Luke's version of the sermon that he preached. This was a sermon he preached not on a mountain, but down on the plain. In a down-to-earth way he said: Blessed are the poor ... woe to you rich. There is enough in the New Testament about the danger of riches and the blessing of poverty to pull up suddenly any preacher of health and wealth and make him go back to his Bible and look more carefully at what he is offering people. Because the offer of health and wealth is exactly what the world wants – they go together. There is no use having wealth if you don't have health. You can't enjoy your wealth if you don't have health. So they go together, and the advertising world knows that and they go for both those. There is more advertising of health products and sale of health products today than ever before in human history. So we are encouraged to get wealth and health in consumerist society. Is the gospel just going to join in that? I don't believe it ought to do so. It is rare for a rich person to enter the kingdom, but it is not impossible. God is the God of the impossible and it happens. But now someone is in the kingdom and rich, they have their own peculiar temptations to face.

Let us sort of see the progression of how wealth can destroy a man. It starts with ambition, an ambition to want to make money, a very common ambition. The ambition is born out of basic emotional needs and the belief that money will meet those needs. Let us look at three basic needs that fallen man has. First, he needs to be secure. He sees money as the path to security. According to Jesus he is a fool, as he says in the teaching about a man who said, "I'll pull my barns down and build bigger and expand my business." Jesus said, "You're a fool". The rich man was totally insecure but planning as if he was going to live forever.

That, I suppose, is the basic temptation to all of us – that we think we are going to live here forever, and that this is our home, and therefore the more secure we are here the better. This emotional need for security means that we have an ambition to make money. Actually, the facts are that the more you have, the more time and energy will be needed to keep it. The more you have, the more you will be afraid of losing. That can be a big worry. The more you have, the more you want. It is extraordinary – it just happens. People who have made enough money to survive the rest of their life in comfort still want more, still want bigger business, still want, still have this ambition. The greater the money you have the more you fear things like inflation or a bust or a recession.

The second emotional need fallen human beings have is to be esteemed by others, to have a built-up reputation so that others will look up to them. It is basically an inferiority complex at the heart of it. People ask, "What's he worth?" – as if the worth of a human being is how much money they have built up. We all tend to this fault if we are not careful, even in Christian circles. That is why James in the second chapter of his letter, says, "If you pay more attention in church to a rich person than a poor person, that is utterly wrong in the sight of God." It is a temptation in Christian circles.

He teaches: "If a rich man comes into your assembly and you say, 'Ah, we've got a special seat for you. Sit here', and a poor man comes in and you say, 'You can stand over there,'" – that is the height of an insult to someone made in the image of God.

But now if a rich man comes into some churches they immediately say, "Would you like to join our giving scheme?" They see a potential customer who will be worth more than some of the others. You might laugh, but it does happen in church. James wrote against that. You are insulting the poor if you give more attention to the rich in your church. Now we all like to be well esteemed and well thought of, and feel good about ourselves as a result. The rich can think, "I must have been more diligent, more careful, more clever, and therefore I'm more superior." That is the danger of having money: that it cures an inferiority complex with a superiority complex, and you are out of one bad thing into another. You tend to look down on those who have been less successful and you tend to have a higher opinion of your own success as compared with others' failures.

The other fallen desire of our nature is to be powerful and to control other people. You make money to give you that power. Money is power; it is power to control other people. Big money is big control. Now all that is the result of the ambition to make money, but the ambition soon fades and becomes an addiction. If you have started living to make money, if you have fallen for the ambition to make money, it won't be long before you can't stop – it has become a drug; it has become like an addiction.

There was a man in England who made his money dealing with cattle, buying and selling them. Eventually, the stress and the strain of it all took its toll and he simply had a collapse. He went to a doctor, a special private doctor (of course he had the money). The doctor said, "You've got to get away from your job. You've got to go right away and take a holiday, and take a complete rest." He decided to go to a well-known hotel down in the southwest of England.

As he checked in at reception, he said to the man behind the desk, "By the way, you don't know anybody around here who's got some cattle to sell, do you?" He had become an addict. He couldn't help it. He just had to go on and on making money, and he had more than enough for himself and his family and everybody else, and there he is, asking on the first minute of his rest, "Is there anyone who can sell some cattle to me?" It can become an obsession, a driving force, and you will go on after you have made all the money you need because you can't stop it. It has become an addiction, a chain of habit, and invariably, such people overreach themselves and go one step too far and buy too many businesses and things begin to collapse.

There are two opposites in the Bible which I want to mention to you now. One is absolutely forbidden by God in the Ten Commandments, and it is covetousness – simple greed. God is absolutely against greed, wanting more, wanting more, wanting more – sheer greed. The opposite of that vice is the virtue of contentment. That is why Paul says that "Godliness with contentment is great profit". It is variously translated, more mildly in some translations, but that is what the Greek word he uses means. That puts it right in the commercial language. Contentment comes from gratitude. Covetousness is greed, but contentment is gratitude.

There is a famous text in Philippians which says, "I can do all things through Christ who strengthens me." I want you to think about something that you could do through Christ who strengthens you that you couldn't do without him. Just think of anything that you can do through Christ who strengthens you. Pause while you think of something.

Now let me ask you a second question. Were you thinking of money? In fact, that text is all about money. It is about managing on your income. Here is the context of the text.

Paul is saying: I've learned how to be poor and how to be rich; I have learned how to have low income and a high income. I have learned to be content whether I have much or little, because I can do all things through Christ who strengthens me. What a text for today, as we struggle to live within our income, and all of us can do that. *Contentment*— Paul says: If I have a lot of money coming in or if I have a little coming in I've learned to be content with what comes in. I can manage on my income.

Which do you think is easier – to be poor and content or to be rich and content? Have you ever thought about that? In the people I've met, I have found it is harder to be rich and content. I have found more contentment among the poor. When I was in India I met many of the poorest of the poor, and you know they looked happier than the rich people I met. There was a contentment – I was amazed. How can you be content like that when you put your baby to sleep in the gutter alongside the road? How can you be content? And yet there is more contentment among the poor. That is a fact. But Paul teaches: I have learned to be content whatever. If there is a lot of money coming in, I can handle that; if there is a little money coming in I can handle that too, because I can do all things through Christ who strengthens me. That is the meaning of that text, and it is to do with money. Of course it can be applied to other areas, but that is the one that it is applied to in Scripture.

Ambition to make money becoming an addiction that you can't stop – and the final position is adoration. Money becomes your god, and there is a Bible word for that god. It is mammon. Jesus said, "You cannot serve God and mammon." If money has become your god, you cannot serve God, it is an utter impossibility. So if money is what you adore and give your life to, you cannot serve God, it is an utter impossibility, an incompatibility. Consider Exodus

16:8. It is when they lived on manna, and there is a verse in the middle of all that, "He who gathered much did not have too much, and he who gathered little did not have too little. Each gathered as much as he needed." Isn't that a lovely little text? I believe in that single verse you have got God's ideal for society. Both are content and both have enough. On the Friday of course they all gathered twice the amount, because on the Sabbath they didn't go out to gather manna so they were allowed by God to gather twice as much on the Friday to see them through the Saturday. God supplied twice as much on the Friday – isn't that interesting?

In the years when the land had to lie fallow every seventh year, God gave them a bumper crop in the sixth year. God honoured the fallow year giving the land a rest, and gave them twice as much the year before. God was approving his land getting a rest from producing crops.

Well now that is *having* and *keeping* money. What about spending it? Think again about that text I have given you, "I can do all things through Christ...." You can live on your income. You are content with a lot or a little. But that is something you have to learn, it doesn't come easily. You learn contentment, and Paul learned. We live in a consumerist society that is constantly saying, "Live up to your income and beyond it and we'll help you to have things that you can't afford." A mortgage is not a debt. You have borrowed money to buy a house and you have paid back that money with interest. That is not a debt. It only becomes a debt if you don't pay it back on the month. Credit society encourages you to buy now and pay later—in Britain, that may be to buy furniture and not pay anything for it for a year, by which time it is probably worn out. But people are tempted to buy special sofas for their lounge because they don't need to pay a penny for a whole year. That is a real temptation.

Or if you buy a car, taking out a loan for it, you can have

it at nought percent interest. It tempts you to buy a bigger car than you could otherwise have afforded. But that is now the grip of society, and it takes a strong Christian faith to resist it. How we spend our money, what has trapped too many people in Britain, even Christians. The same thing trapped people in Texas, wealthy Christians. I met many wealthy Christians in Texas who are now bankrupt. What had happened was in the boom years they had borrowed more and more money to do more and more business, then, when the boom years ended, there were many crashes among Christian businessmen there, who were in despair.

You see, if you are not careful, you take out a mortgage for a house that is really bigger than you would have bought, and in the good times when interest is low and the bank rate is down you look ahead and say, "I can afford to repay that," and then the climate changes. Bank rates go up, interest rates go up, and that left many people in Britain in a real hole. Others have been trapped in a house that has lost value, and they have almost a negative mortgage to pay off, which they can never pay off. They can't sell the house now because it is not worth what it was and the mortgage interest has gone up.

When you buy a house and take a mortgage out, don't buy the top house you can afford at the moment and take out a mortgage that you will not be able to repay. That means taking out a mortgage where the interest and repayments will be within your ability when things go bad. I know it is a fairly fine judgment, but what I'm trying to say is that most people who buy a house in Britain buy one as high as they can afford with the present interest rates. That is just laying themselves wide open to getting into debt when they can't repay.

I want to make that quite clear that it is legitimate to borrow money to buy something and repay it with proper interest. What goes wrong is when you can't afford to repay it and you get behind with the repayment. You are now in debt. According to the Bible, debt is a sin. We are exhorted to keep ourselves out of debt.

But I have been asking Christian congregations in England, "How many of you are in debt?" and the average has been two-thirds of the congregation. I have explained that having a mortgage is not being in debt, or having a monthly account for your petrol is not to be in debt. But it is to be in debt if you have reached the end of the month and you can't pay for your petrol. Yet two-thirds of the professing Christians in England are now in debt. Why is debt a sin? Because it is stealing and one of the clear commandments of God is: "Thou shalt not steal."

But people don't realise there are two ways of stealing. If I rob you of your purse or copy your credit card number and take money out of your bank account, I am stealing money from you, and no Christian would dream of doing that, I hope. But if I owe someone money and I don't pay, I am stealing from them the money I borrowed. I am stealing from them money that belongs to them on the date of repayment. I am withholding money from them that they should have. It is still stealing. Christians don't steal. Ephesians says, "Let him who stole steal no more, and let him earn enough to support himself and give to the poor." So debt is a sin.

You have probably heard of the Keswick Convention. It is usually heard around the world. It was probably the biggest Christian convention in England at one time. For many years since 1875, this convention has been held in the Lake District, the most beautiful part of England. Among the lakes is this town of Keswick. The Keswick Convention is so famous that I find Keswick conventions all over the world. They have copied that convention and kept the name. They are not in Keswick, but they call themselves "The Keswick Convention."

On the first Keswick Convention, when all the Christians gathered to hear the Word of God and praise God and rejoice in their salvation, the post office in Keswick ran out of what we call "postal orders". That is an order that can transfer money by mail to someone else. Why did the Keswick post office run right out of postal orders? The preacher in the Keswick Convention had told people to pay their debts. The post office had a queue of Christians buying postal orders to send off to pay their debts. I like that kind of Christianity, it is down-to-earth, it is practical, and it was a witness to the Keswick postal workers that things were happening in the big tent of the Keswick Convention.

To make provision for the future is not wrong. When the Bible says, "make it your ambition to be dependent on nobody", I think that also means to make provision for yourself for your life. Especially if you are in an occupation that has compulsory retirement at a certain age, you don't want to be a beggar now and you don't want to be a beggar then. It is right to provide a reasonable pension by paying in during your working life. But there are some people who are paying in at an extraordinary rate so that they will have a pension that will make them wealthy, and then they can spend it all on themselves when they don't need to go to work. There is a careful balance of how much you will need and how much you ought to lay by. But saving money like that is a Christian thing to do. John Wesley used to advise all his converts, "Get all you can, waive all you can, and give all you can." He found, of course, that the Methodist converts who were coming out of a decadent Britain, the early Methodists, were described as "snowdrops growing on a foul rubbish heap." Of course they had spent a fortune on gambling and drinking, and when they became Christians they stopped both and found themselves with money.

I heard a Methodist of today once say he was asked in an open-air meeting, "Do you believe Jesus can change water into wine?" This Methodist, who was a coal miner and a dear friend of mine, had been a horse race "bookie" (who took bets) before he had been a Christian, then he became a coal miner. Then this question was thrown at him, "Do you believe Jesus can change water into wine?" He replied, "I don't know about that, but he has changed beer into furniture into my house"—which is a perfect answer! But that has happened to many people who have been converted.

Wesley's biggest problem was that when he preached and got so many converts they became middle-class and had more money than they had ever had before, because they no longer spent it in sinful ways. His problem then was that the danger of riches set in. We are stewards of our money. All the silver and the gold in the world belongs to God and we are only stewards of it. The biggest problem of tithing is that you think ninety percent belongs to you. Dare I repeat that? The biggest problem with tithing is that it makes you think the rest is yours. It is all God's actually. Whether you give it directly to Christian work or to the poor or whatever, it is all his and he will be auditor of our accounts one day. That needs to be thought about, doesn't it – the danger of tithing?

Tithing was a tax in the Old Testament. Many people think the Jews paid a tenth of their income. They didn't. They paid twenty-five percent of their income to the Lord because they had two tithes to pay. You read the Old Testament again. They had two tithes to pay and they had about five percent more than that to pay for other things that God wanted. The average Jew had to pay twenty-five percent of his income to the Lord as well as a seventh of his time, and those were compulsory. We are not under the Mosaic covenant. We are not under the law, and always be suspicious of a church that tells you how much you ought to pay. That is your decision in the new covenant – it is your responsibility in the new covenant.

So we must move on now to *giving*, getting rid of your money and how to do that. I remember a rich man saying this to me: "I do make a lot of money, but it doesn't stick to my fingers." That was an interesting comment and he was a good, dear Christian. "It doesn't stick to my fingers." God is generous – so generous that we have a special word for his generosity, the word "grace". We are to be generous. We can't really give anything to God himself because he doesn't need anything from us.

Think of that verse in Psalm 50 which says: "'If I were hungry I wouldn't tell you,' says the Lord." What a lovely text. He goes on to say, "The cattle on a thousand hills are mine and if I want some beef I would take it." But we are to be generous. It is to be a mark of the people of God that the more they love God and know God, the more generous they will be. Jesus said, "Where your treasure is, that's where your heart will be," and he was talking about investing in heaven. That is the best bank to invest in because neither moth nor rust can get into that, as Jesus said.

I was invited to go and speak in the stock exchange in London to all the stockbrokers. They insisted on my sending a title of my talk ahead of me to advertise. With my tongue in cheek I said, "The title of my talk will be: You Can't Take it with You, and if You Could it Would Burn." They didn't like that title at all and they immediately demanded another. So I said, "Alright, I'll change the title." I gave them this title: "How to Invest Your Money Beyond the Grave". They were all concerned with investing money before the grave, and with their retirement before the grave. None of them were thinking about investing money beyond the grave, except for some of them who were Christians. But Jesus told us how to do that. Luke 16 is the chapter for you to read. It is all about money from beginning to end. It begins with the parable of the dishonest steward, which has puzzled a lot of people. Jesus praises a man who got out of financial difficulty by cheating on his boss. It is an extraordinary story. I am sure you have read it and puzzled about it – it seems an immoral story. Here is a man who was an agent for a wealthy boss and he collected wages from a lot of people, wages in the form of goods really, because they were farmers. The rich man had a big estate and there were tenants and he was the agent who would collect the rents in the form of oil or grain or whatever for his boss. Now he was already fiddling, he was already pocketing more than he should, and the rich man heard about this and told him, "I'm giving you the sack. The end of the month comes, that's it, you're out. You've been fiddling; you've been helping yourself to what belongs to me."

That man thought, "What can I do now? I'm not likely to get another job. I won't get a reference from this boss. I'm not going to beg, that's humiliating." He hit on a great scheme. He went to the tenants of his boss and said, "How much do you owe my boss?"

A tenant would say, "A thousand barrels of olive oil." He would say, "Well, give me the paper from the boss that told you owe that." And he took the paper and he crossed out a thousand and he put five hundred. He said, "That's all you owe the boss." He went around all the tenants cutting down what they owed to his boss. And Jesus said that man has something to teach Christians. You would have thought, "What?" Well, he was using his last remaining time to make friends who would look after him later. He was doing everybody a favour that would make them think better of him. They were happy to cut down what they owed, so they would all be his friends when he was sacked and would help him.

Now Jesus says that man was shrewd. He wasn't commending the way he did it. But he was saying two things about that man. First, he was thinking more about the future than the present. He could have walked away with everything he had collected and gone. But he didn't. He used it to do a favour. He was thinking about the future rather than the present and he was more concerned with people than things. He could have collected it all in a hurry and disappeared. But he was more concerned to make friends than to make money. He was more concerned to provide for his future than for the present. It would have been a very short-term policy to collect all the rent and go. That would have been disaster. He was shrewd enough to do something that was helpful, whereby he would be welcomed by other people. Had he walked off with a lot, immediately nobody would have given him any time or attention. They would have said, "Don't touch that man." But he so used what opportunity he had. Jesus taught that is shrewdness, that is right thinking. If the children of darkness can think that way, then let the children of light think that way and plan for the future rather than the present and plan to make friends rather than money. He was teaching: use dirty money yourself to make friends who will welcome you into heaven. That is learning the lesson from that man.

The steward was a bad man and it was a bad thing he did, but he was shrewd enough to think of the future and to make friends in the future. The teaching was: use your money like that to make friends who will welcome you into heaven and you have learned the lesson that I've taught you. It is quite an extraordinary parable. But Jesus is using a bad man to teach good people something that they should do. He went on to talk about money a great deal, and that you cannot serve God and mammon. He went on until the Pharisees, who were lovers of money, laughed at him. They said, "You don't know what you're talking about." They were successful businessmen and Jesus was obviously not. He was a poor man who had nothing much to his name. They mocked him and he said, "You mock me, but I'm telling you the truth." He finished up by telling them, "You are divorcing your wives and remarrying and that's against God." It's rich people who happily change their partner and can afford to pay alimony. Poor people can't afford to divorce, some of them, though they would if they could. That is where Jesus' teaching on divorce and remarriage came in.

Then he went on to another story of a rich man, so rich that there were ornamental gates to the drive leading up to his house – that is the word he uses. This rich man had fine clothes and a good table of food, and he wasn't bad, it was just that he was rich and comfortable. At his gate, just outside the gate, in the gutter sat a poor man called Lazarus, the only man Jesus ever named in a parable. "Lazarus" means loved by God. Nobody else loved the poor man. His body was covered with ulcers which wild dogs came and licked. Dogs in the Bible are always wild. Dogs in the Middle East are wild dogs, they are not pets.

The dogs came and licked his sores and he would have loved to go into the rich house and get under the dining room table and eat the bits of bread that there were there, because the rich people then cleaned their hands on a lump of bread. If you have ever made bread you know that kneading the dough with your hands makes them beautifully clean, all the dirt has gone into the dough. So that is what they used to do. They would take a lump of bread at the end of a meal and rub it all over their hands until their hands were nice and clean, and throw the bit of bread under the table. That beggar would have given anything to go under the rich man's table and eat the dirty bits of bread. It is a vivid contrast between someone who was rich and someone who was poor. In the story they die and the rich man finds himself in a very uncomfortable place. He can see in a vision the beggar, and angels are escorting him to Abraham's presence and Abraham embraces him. The rich man is in fire, hot and dry, and he begs, "Father Abraham, send Lazarus and dip his finger in water and let me suck his finger, I'm so thirsty in this dreadful place." It is a vivid picture. The situation of both men is now totally reversed. Abraham said to the rich man, "I'm sorry, we can't do this, there is a great gulf between you and here and it can't be crossed, it's fixed forever."

He thought of something else: "Then please send someone back to my house where my brothers are still living and tell them what it's like here."

Abraham says, "Even if someone went back from the dead to tell them they wouldn't believe," and he finished up by saying, "They've got a Bible in the house, let them read it."

It is an amazing story. The rich man had not committed a crime. He had no vices. He wasn't a bad man. What was wrong with him? Well, if you read the story, three things. He spent his money on himself, not on anybody who needed it. So he indulged himself. He was indifferent to others, and therefore didn't give his money away, and he was independent of God. He had a Bible but never read it. That's all. He wasn't a great sinner. But that was enough to decide his eternal future, a fixed future. He had never thought of life beyond the grave, his only thought was how to be comfortable here.

That is the lesson of that. Think of the ultimate future. Jesus is saying: think of beyond the grave; learn, like the unjust steward, to make friends who will welcome you to heaven. In other words, spend your money in such a way that people will greet you in heaven and say, "I'm so thankful for your money because it got me here." It is as simple as that then – the story of the two rich and poor men.

Solomon, when he began his reign, was offered by God a choice: I can give you wealth or wisdom, which do you want? Solomon as a young man was very wise and he said, "I'd rather have wisdom." So God said to him, "I'll give you both." He gave him wisdom the next day when two women were arguing over a baby. They had each had a baby and overnight one had had what we call, a "cot death" and the baby suffocated and died. When they woke in the morning there was only one live baby and one dead baby. They looked much alike, as babies do, and they both claimed the dead baby was the other woman's. They came to Solomon to settle the argument.

Can you imagine any worse situation than two women arguing over one baby and coming to you to decide who it should belong to? Solomon showed the next day that God had answered his prayer and given him wisdom. He said, "The answer is cut the baby in half and give half to you and half to you." The real mother immediately said, "Give it to the other woman!" She would rather have her baby alive and someone else looking after it. Solomon said, "You're the mother. Yours is the baby." How wise. If only Solomon had continued like that, but the wealth got hold of him and he built magnificent buildings, magnificent palaces. He spent money like water. Yes, he built the first big temple, a magnificent place. But he built it with people's money and taxed them so heavily to build that temple that the minute he died there was civil war and ten of the twelve tribes said, "We're going to be independent, we're not having the king in Jerusalem taxing us like Solomon did," and they broke away. The people of God from then on were ten tribes in the north and two in the south. So the king of Jerusalem's kingdom shrank overnight.

They told me in Sunday School that Solomon was the wisest man in the Bible apart from Jesus. Did you think he was wise? He had seven hundred mothers-in-law. Would you say that was wise? Having one is too much for some husbands. But having seven hundred mothers-in-law and three hundred mistresses on top of seven hundred wives – you call that wise? It was utter folly and he paid for it, and the nation paid for it because a nation with a bad king is going to be a bad nation. If only he had stayed with his wisdom.

For the rest of his life he had great wisdom for other people but he never lived by it himself. He married an Egyptian, a Gentile, and built for her an Egyptian palace. (An Egyptologist has discovered Solomon's buildings and identified them.)

If you want to know what Solomon did with his money, he tells you. Solomon wrote three books in your Bible, and you can tell what age he is by the book. He wrote a book when he had sixty wives, so he was then quite early in his career. The girl he had met and sang the Song of Solomon to, he said, was the most beautiful of them all and far better than all the other sixty queens. He was still a young man. He is full of love for this girl – and there is not a word about God in the Song of Solomon, and not a word about salvation or prayer or anything spiritual at all. It is just a love song for a girl. There is more meaning to it than that for us, but for him it is just a love song.

The Bible says he wrote 1005 songs. We have only got the five. A thousand have been lost. I think that was God's way of saying: I had one wife for you and you had a thousand women, and you sang a love song for each – you composed and sang a new pop song for each of them and I've rejected a thousand of them, I'll include five in my word.

But Solomon was a young man then, so full of love for a girl that he had no time for God. That happens to a lot of people, and a girl walks into their life and she is the "goddess" for a bit.

When he wrote the book of Proverbs, how old do you think Solomon is? Because the book of Proverbs says, "Now son, be careful about the women, they'll get you if you're not careful." How old is he? He is middle-aged and he is collecting wise proverbs, having learned the hard way. I was in a home once where the teenage girl in the family said to her mother, "What did you do at my age that makes you so worried about me?" I thought, "That's a devastating question for a parent to be asked." So here is Solomon in middle age saying, "Now son, you keep off the women." I don't know how he dares to say it.

Then you turn to the book of Ecclesiastes. How old is Solomon now? He says, "Remember your Creator in the days of your youth before the eyes are dim and the legs shake and you can't hear the sounds of the birds." You can see him as an old man, "Remember your Creator when you're young" – he is speaking as an old man who has reached the end of the road, and the book of Ecclesiastes is one of the most depressing books in the Bible. Yet when I preached my way through it I saw more conversions than perhaps for any other book, because it faces people with how they will feel when they have reached the end of the road. Here is one passage:

I thought in my heart, "Come now, I will test you with pleasure to find out what is good." But that also proved to me meaningless. "Laughter," I said, "is foolish. And what does pleasure accomplish?" I tried cheering myself up with wine, and embracing folly—my mind still guiding me with wisdom. I wanted to see what was worthwhile for men to do under heaven during the few days of their life. I undertook great projects: I built houses for myself and planted vineyards. I made gardens and parks and planted all kinds of fruit trees in them. I made reservoirs to water groves of flourishing trees. I bought male and female slaves and I had other slaves who were born in my house. I also owned more herds and flocks than anyone in Jerusalem before me. I amassed silver and gold for myself, and the treasure of kings and provinces. I acquired men and women singers, and a harem as well—the delights of the heart of man. I became greater by far than anyone in Jerusalem before me. In all this my wisdom stayed with me. I denied myself nothing my eyes desired; I refused my heart no pleasure. My heart took delight in all my work, and this was the reward for all my labour. Yet when I surveyed all that my hands had done and what I had toiled to achieve, everything was meaningless, a chasing after the wind; nothing was gained.

That is the sad testimony of the richest man in Old Testament history and what he did with all his money. His summary at the end was: I gained nothing. I have used that book. It is an amazing book, Ecclesiastes. It finishes with that appeal to young people, "Remember your Creator in the days of your youth." It is the one thing he had not done – when he was young and in love, God didn't get a look in. Then he goes on to describe old age, what it does to your teeth, even when the teeth are few and the eyes are dim and the legs are weak. Then, finally, he says, "Meaningless, meaningless, everything is meaningless." Of course he didn't know about the life beyond the grave. They didn't know, most of them in the Old Testament. So he was judging life here. I suppose the saddest thing is to get to the end of your life and feeling that you have not achieved anything worthwhile.

That is in your Bible to pull you up with a jerk: if you become a servant of mammon and you do many things with your money, but you reach the end of the life with nothing gained. You could weep for poor old Solomon, but that is what happened to him. I am thankful that Solomon wrote it down and tells us how he felt after the richest lifetime you could imagine.

ABOUT
DAVID
PAWSON

A speaker and author with uncompromising faithfulness to the Holy Scriptures, David brings clarity and a message of urgency to Christians to uncover hidden treasures in God's Word.

Born in England in 1930, David began his career with a degree in Agriculture from Durham University. When God intervened and called him to become a Minister, he completed an MA in Theology at Cambridge University and served as a Chaplain in the Royal Air Force for three years. He moved on to pastor several churches, including the Millmead Centre in Guildford, which became a model for many UK church leaders. In 1979, the Lord led him into an international ministry. His current itinerant ministry is predominantly to church leaders. David and his wife Enid currently reside in the county of Hampshire in the UK.

Over the years, he has written a large number of books, booklets, and daily reading notes. His extensive and very accessible overviews of the books of the Bible have been published and recorded in *Unlocking the Bible*. Millions of copies of his teachings have been distributed in more than 120 countries, providing a solid biblical foundation.

He is reputed to be the "most influential Western preacher in China" through the broadcast of his best-selling *Unlocking the Bible* series into every Chinese province by Good TV. In the UK, David's teachings are often broadcast on Revelation TV.

Countless believers worldwide have also benefited from his generous decision in 2011 to make available his extensive audio video teaching library free of charge at www.davidpawson.org and we have recently uploaded all of David's video to a dedicated channel on www.youtube.com

TAKE A LOOK AT YOUTUBE
www.youtube.com/user/DavidPawsonMinistry

THE EXPLAINING SERIES
BIBLICAL TRUTHS SIMPLY EXPLAINED

If you have been blessed reading this book, there are more available in the series. Please register to download more booklets for free by visiting **www.explainingbiblicaltruth.global**

Other booklets in the *Explaining* series will include:
The Amazing Story of Jesus
The Resurrection: *The Heart of Christianity*
Studying the Bible
Being Anointed and Filled with the Holy Spirit
New Testament Baptism
How to study a book of the Bible: Jude
The Key Steps to Becoming a Christian
What the Bible says about Money
What the Bible says about Work
Grace – *Undeserved Favour, Irresistible Force or Unconditional Forgiveness?*
Eternally secure? – *What the Bible says about being saved*
De-Greecing the Church – The impact of Greek thinking on Christian beliefs
Three texts often taken out of context: *Expounding the truth and exposing error*
The Trinity
The Truth about Christmas

They will also be avaiable to purchase as print copies from:
Amazon or **www.thebookdepository.com**

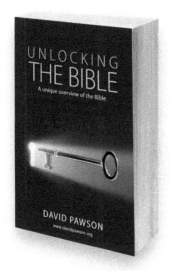

UNLOCKING THE BIBLE

A unique overview of both the Old and New Testaments, from internationally acclaimed evangelical speaker and author David Pawson. *Unlocking the Bible* opens up the Word of God in a fresh and powerful way. Avoiding the small detail of verse by verse studies, it sets out the epic story of God and his people in Israel. The culture, historical background and people are introduced and the teaching applied to the modern world. Eight volumes have been brought into one compact and easy to use guide to cover both the Old and New Testaments in one massive omnibus edition. *The Old Testament: The Maker's Instructions* (The five books of law); *A Land and A Kingdom* (Joshua, Judges, Ruth, 1&2 Samuel, 1&2 Kings); *Poems of Worship and Wisdom* (Psalms, Song of Solomon, Proverbs, Ecclesiastes, Job); *Decline and Fall of an Empire* (Isaiah, Jeremiah and other prophets); *The Struggle to Survive* (Chronicles and prophets of exile); *The New Testament: The Hinge of History* (Mathew, Mark, Luke, John and Acts); *The Thirteenth Apostle* (Paul and his letters); *Through Suffering to Glory* (Hebrews, the letters of James, Peter and Jude, the Book of Revelation). Already an international bestseller.

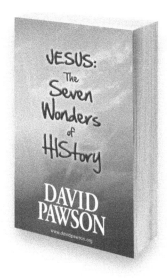

JESUS:
THE SEVEN
WONDERS
OF HISTORY

This book is the result of a lifetime of telling 'the greatest story ever told' around the world. David re-told it to many hundreds of young people in Kansas City, USA, who heard it with uninhibited enthusiasm, 'tweeting' on the internet about 'this cute old English gentleman' even while he was speaking.

Taking the middle section of the Apostles' Creed as a framework, David explains the fundamental facts about Jesus on which the Christian faith is based in a fresh and stimulating way. Both old and new Christians will benefit from this 'back to basics' call and find themselves falling in love with their Lord all over again.

OTHER TEACHINGS
BY DAVID PAWSON

For the most up to date list of David's Books
go to: **www.davidpawsonbooks.com**

To purchase David's Teachings
go to: **www.davidpawson.com**

Lightning Source UK Ltd.
Milton Keynes UK
UKHW020627030921
389968UK00013B/1487